PIANO SOLO / OPTIONAL CELLO

The Piano Guys
COVERS

10 BLESS THE BROKEN ROAD

2 FIGHT SONG/AMAZING GRACE

14 JESU, JOY OF MAN'S DESIRING

18 LINE UPON LINE

24 SAY SOMETHING

27 A SKY FULL OF STARS

36 THINKING OUT LOUD

40 WHAT ARE WORDS

44 WHEN YOU SAY NOTHING AT ALL

ISBN 978-1-4950-5611-6

HAL•LEONARD®
7777 W. BLUEMOUND RD. P.O. BOX 13819 MILWAUKEE, WI 53213

Visit Hal Leonard Online at
www.halleonard.com

Visit The Piano Guys at
thepianoguys.com

Contact us:
Hal Leonard
7777 West Bluemound Road
Milwaukee, WI 53213
Email: info@halleonard.com

In Europe, contact:
Hal Leonard Europe Limited
42 Wigmore Street
Marylebone, London, W1U 2RN
Email: info@halleonardeurope.com

In Australia, contact:
Hal Leonard Australia Pty. Ltd.
4 Lentara Court
Cheltenham, Victoria, 3192 Australia
Email: info@halleonard.com.au

As performed by The Piano Guys

FIGHT SONG/AMAZING GRACE

Words and Music by RACHEL PLATTEN
and DAVE BASSETT
Arranged by Al van der Beek,
Steven Sharp Nelson and Jon Schmidt

Moderately fast

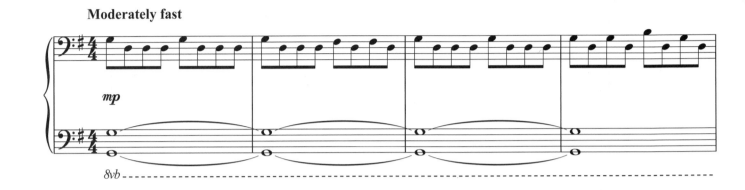

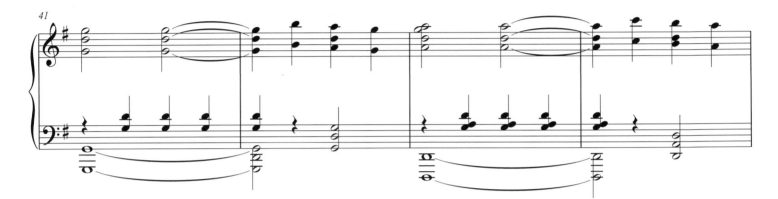

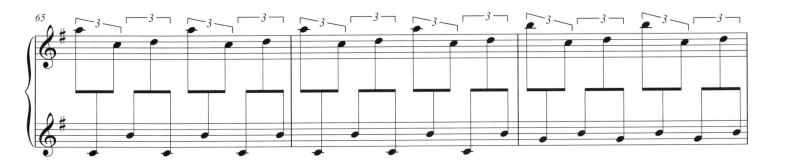

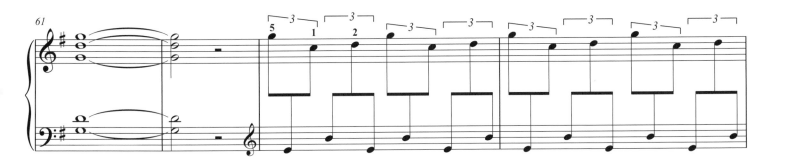

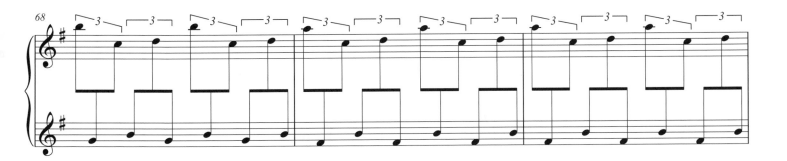

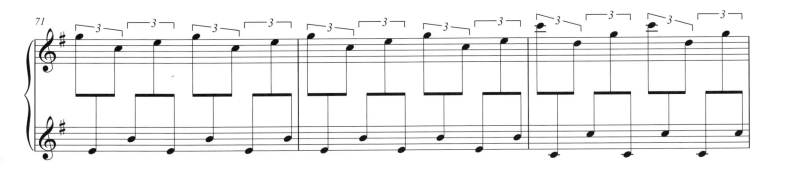

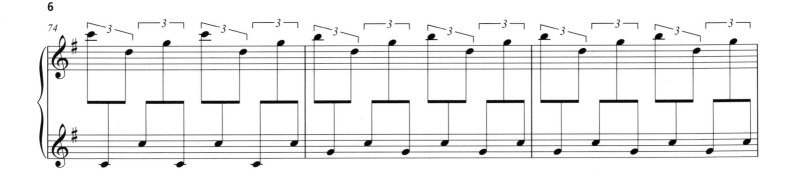

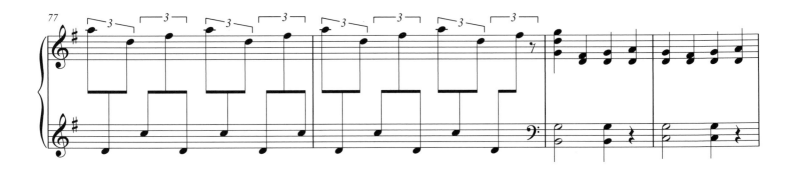

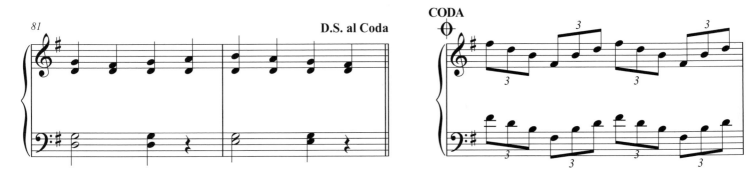

D.S. al Coda

CODA

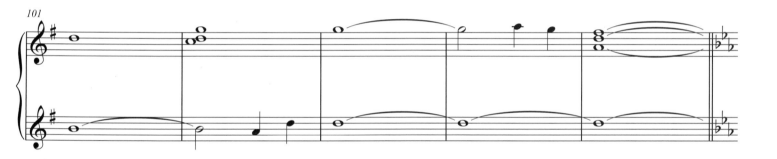

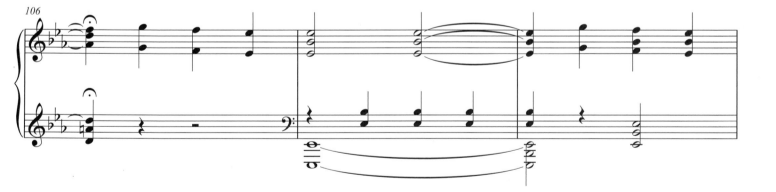

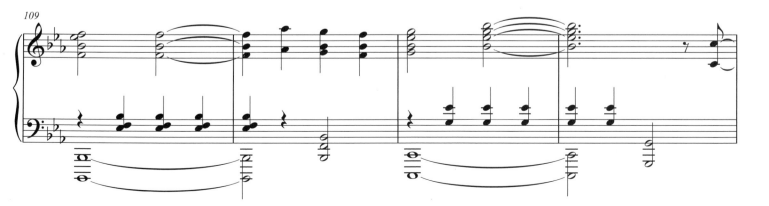

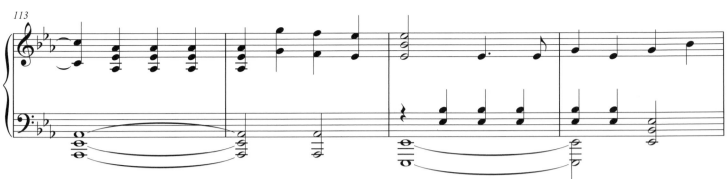

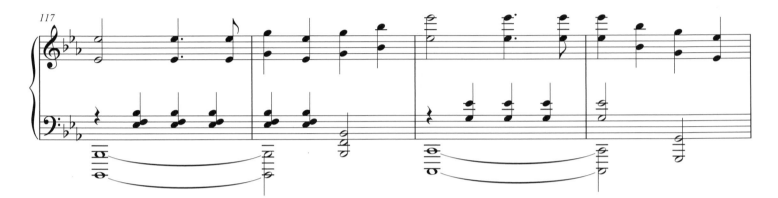

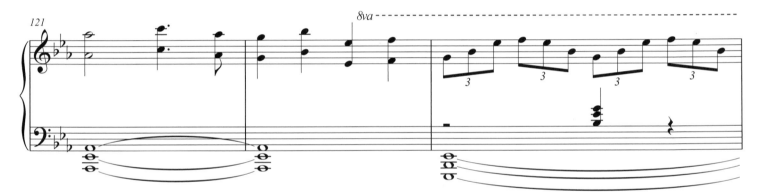

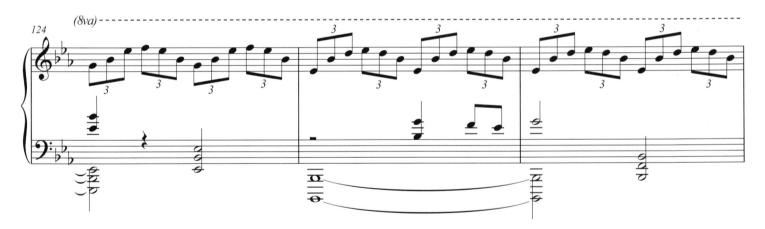

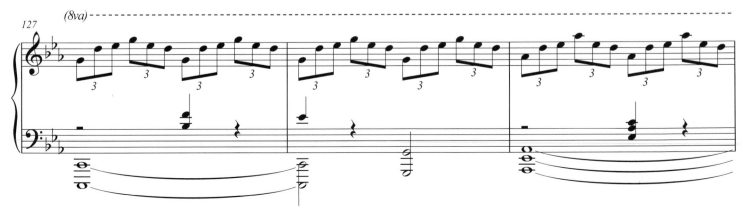

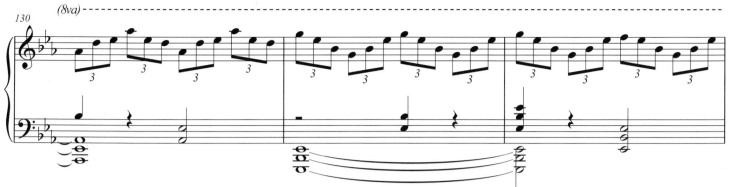

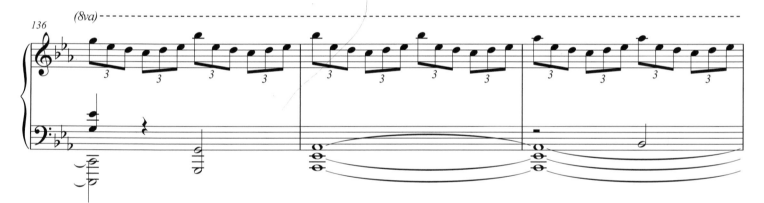

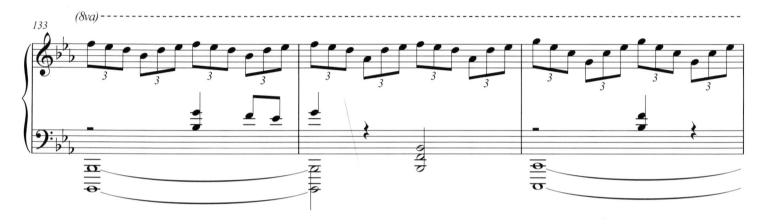

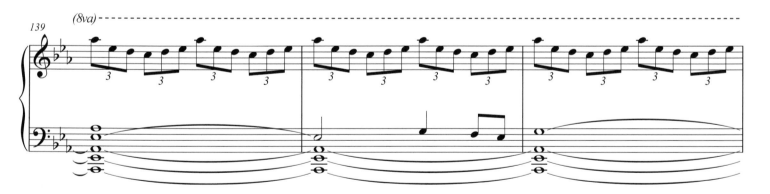

As performed by The Piano Guys

BLESS THE BROKEN ROAD

Words and Music by MARCUS HUMMON,
BOBBY BOYD and JEFF HANNA
Arranged by Jon Schmidt

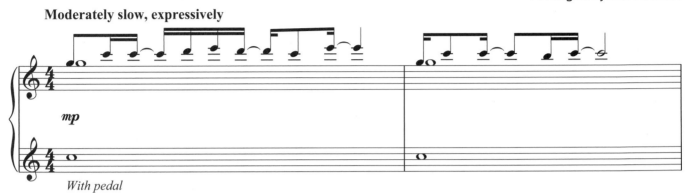

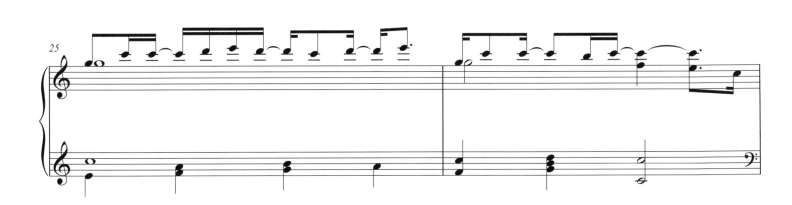

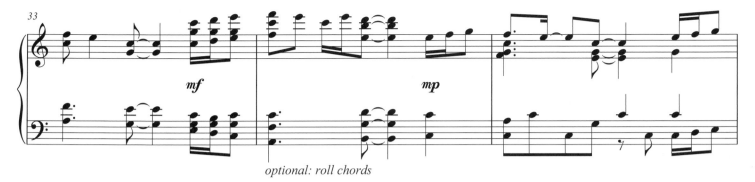

As performed by The Piano Guys

JESU, JOY OF MAN'S DESIRING

By JOHANN SEBASTIAN BACH
Arranged by Jon Schmidt

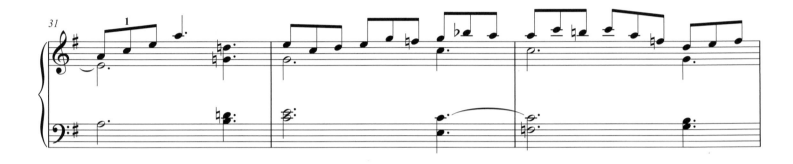

As performed by The Piano Guys

LINE UPON LINE

Words by DOUGLAS STEWART
Music by ALEXIS DE AZEVEDO
Arranged by Jon Schmidt

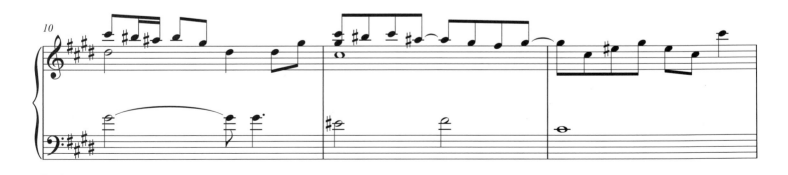

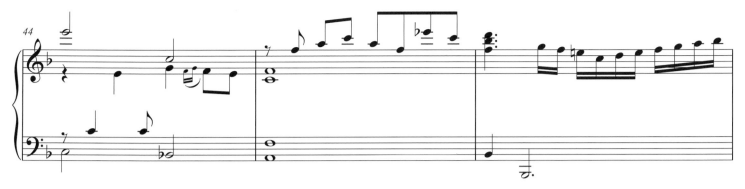

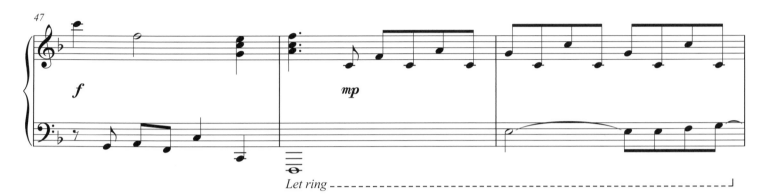

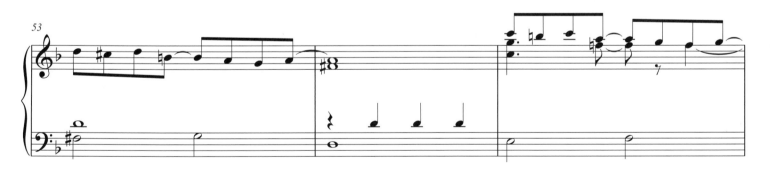

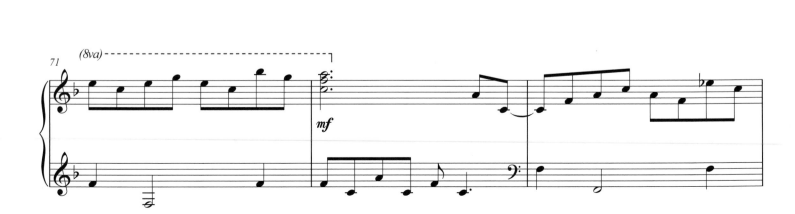

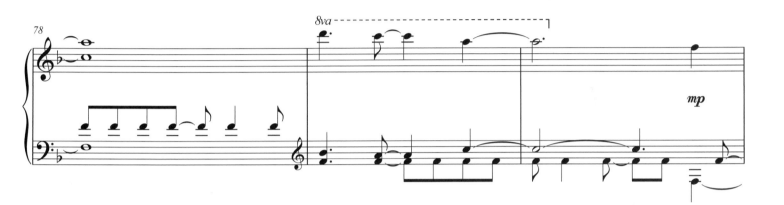

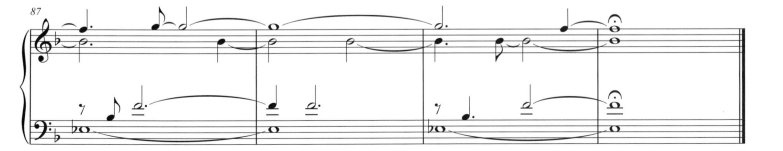

As performed by The Piano Guys

SAY SOMETHING

Words and Music by IAN AXEL,
CHAD VACCARINO and MIKE CAMPBELL
Arranged by Shane Mickelsen
and Jon Schmidt

Moderately, in 4

The PianoGuys
COVERS

5   BLESS THE BROKEN ROAD

2   FIGHT SONG/AMAZING GRACE

6   JESU, JOY OF MAN'S DESIRING

7   LINE UPON LINE

8   SAY SOMETHING

10 A SKY FULL OF STARS

9   THINKING OUT LOUD

12 WHAT ARE WORDS

13 WHEN YOU SAY NOTHING AT ALL

ISBN 978-1-4950-5611-6

HAL•LEONARD®

7777 W. BLUEMOUND RD. P.O. BOX 13819 MILWAUKEE, WI 53213

Visit Hal Leonard Online at
www.halleonard.com

Visit The Piano Guys at
thepianoguys.com

Contact us:
Hal Leonard
7777 West Bluemound Road
Milwaukee, WI 53213
Email: info@halleonard.com

In Europe, contact:
Hal Leonard Europe Limited
42 Wigmore Street
Marylebone, London, W1U 2RN
Email: info@halleonardeurope.com

In Australia, contact:
Hal Leonard Australia Pty. Ltd.
4 Lentara Court
Cheltenham, Victoria, 3192 Australia
Email: info@halleonard.com.au

HL00155254

Cello

As performed by The Piano Guys

FIGHT SONG/AMAZING GRACE

Words and Music by RACHEL PLATTEN
and DAVE BASSETT
Arranged by Al van der Beek,
Steven Sharp Nelson and Jon Schmidt

Cello

As performed by The Piano Guys

BLESS THE BROKEN ROAD

Words and Music by MARCUS HUMMON,
BOBBY BOYD and JEFF HANNA
Arranged by Jon Schmidt

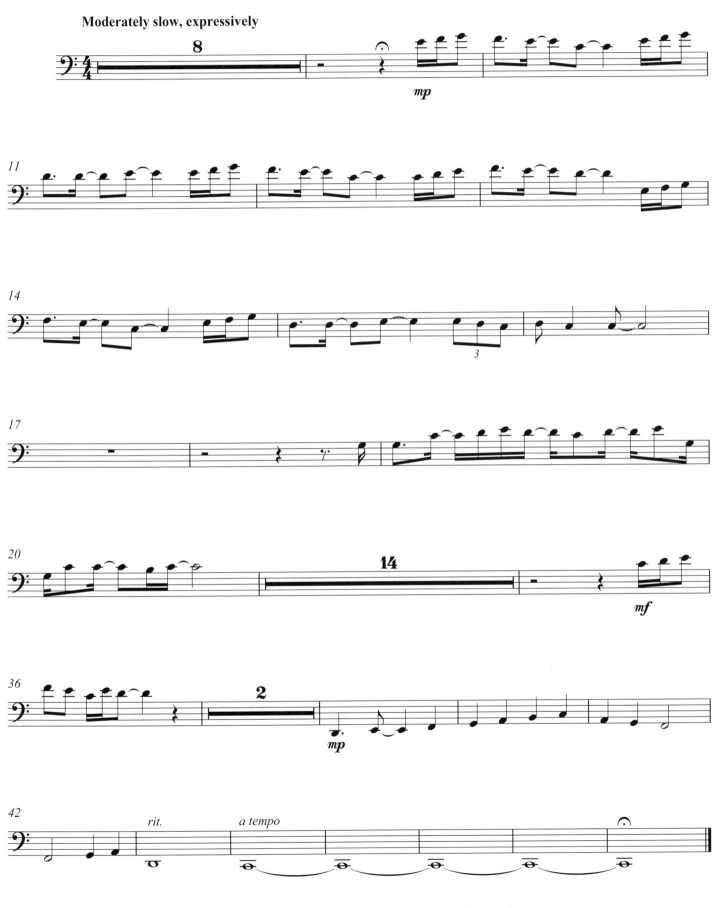

Cello

As performed by The Piano Guys

JESU, JOY OF MAN'S DESIRING

By JOHANN SEBASTIAN BACH
Arranged by Jon Schmidt

As performed by The Piano Guys

LINE UPON LINE

Words by DOUGLAS STEWART
Music by ALEXIS DE AZEVEDO
Arranged by Jon Schmidt

Cello

As performed by The Piano Guys

SAY SOMETHING

Words and Music by IAN AXEL,
CHAD VACCARINO and MIKE CAMPBELL
Arranged by Shane Mickelsen
and Jon Schmidt

As performed by The Piano Guys

THINKING OUT LOUD

Words and Music by ED SHEERAN
and AMY WADGE
Arranged by Shane Mickelsen
and Jon Schmidt

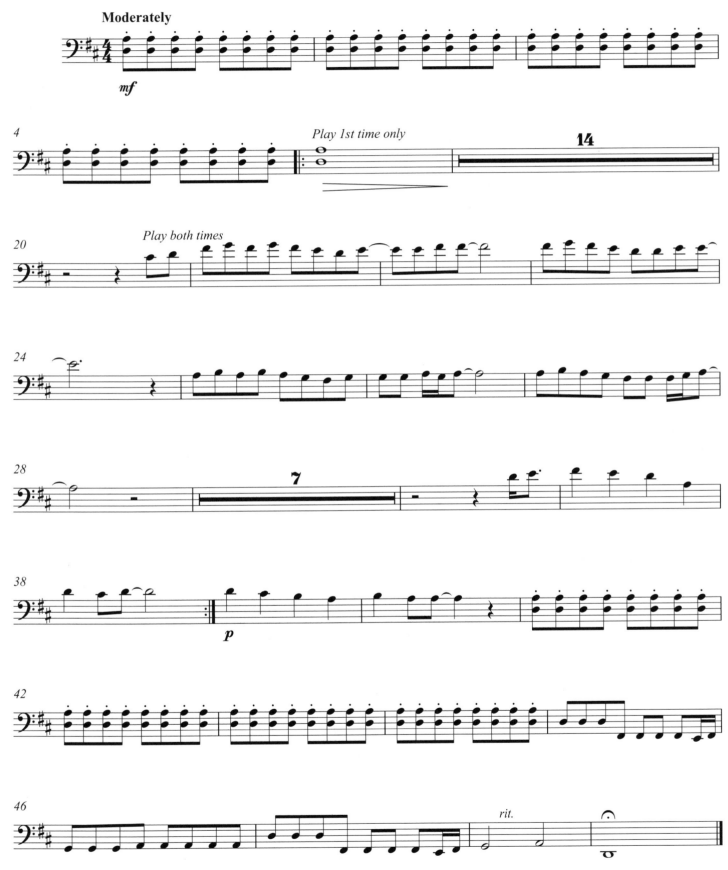

Cello

As performed by The Piano Guys

A SKY FULL OF STARS

Words and Music by GUY BERRYMAN,
JON BUCKLAND, WILL CHAMPION,
CHRIS MARTIN and TIM BERGLING
Arranged by Steven Sharp Nelson
and Jon Schmidt

Cello

As performed by The Piano Guys

WHAT ARE WORDS

Words and Music by RODNEY JERKINS,
ANDRE LINDAL and LAUREN CHRISTY
Arranged by Tom Anderson
and Jon Schmidt

WHEN YOU SAY NOTHING AT ALL

As performed by The Piano Guys

Words and Music by DON SCHLITZ
and PAUL OVERSTREET
Arranged by Jon Schmidt

small hand
omit G

rit.

As performed by The Piano Guys

A SKY FULL OF STARS

Words and Music by GUY BERRYMAN,
JON BUCKLAND, WILL CHAMPION,
CHRIS MARTIN and TIM BERGLING
Arranged by Steven Sharp Nelson
and Jon Schmidt

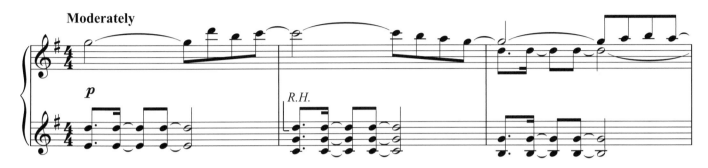

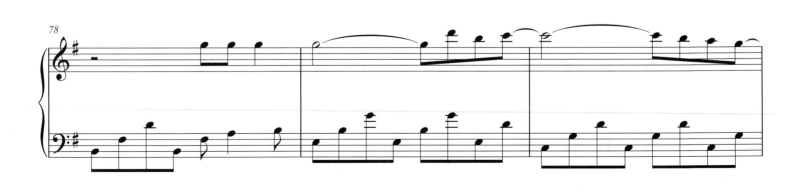

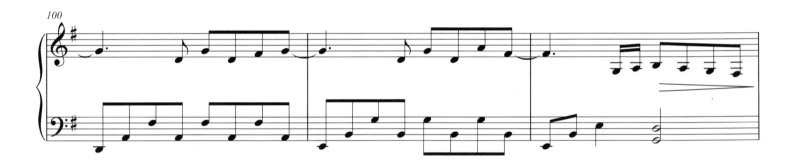

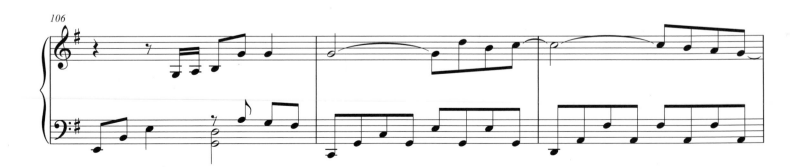

As performed by The Piano Guys

THINKING OUT LOUD

Words and Music by ED SHEERAN
and AMY WADGE
Arranged by Shane Mickelsen
and Jon Schmidt

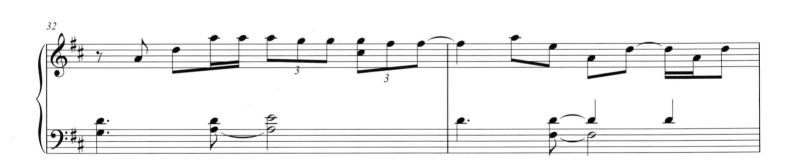

As performed by The Piano Guys

WHAT ARE WORDS

Words and Music by RODNEY JERKINS,
ANDRE LINDAL and LAUREN CHRISTY
Arranged by Tom Anderson
and Jon Schmidt

Slowly, freely

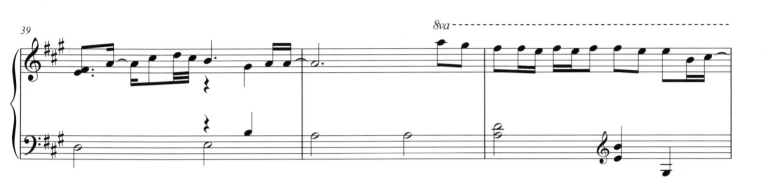

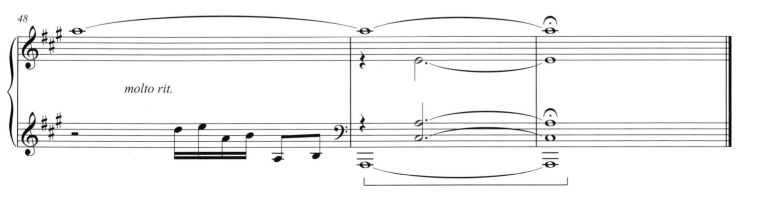

As performed by The Piano Guys

WHEN YOU SAY NOTHING AT ALL

Words and Music by DON SCHLITZ
and PAUL OVERSTREET
Arranged by Jon Schmidt

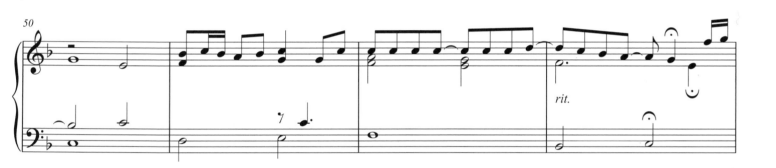

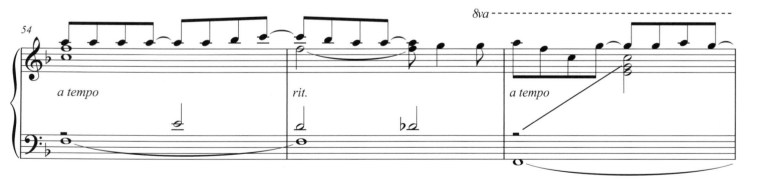

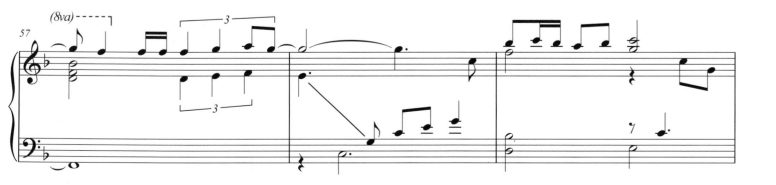

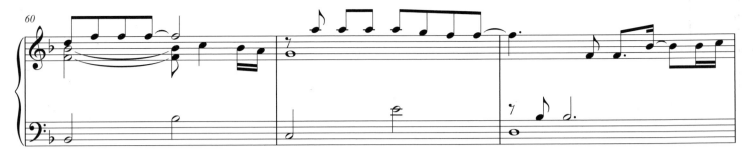

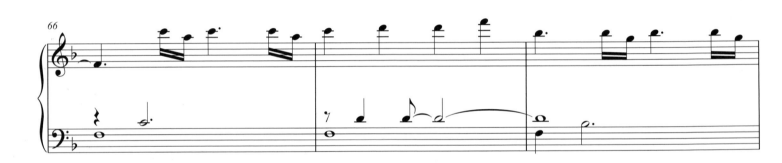